FRENCH CHIC

A French Woman's Guide To Dress Elegantly And Live Effortlessly Chic

SOPHIE CLAIRE

TABLE OF CONTENTS

FRENCH CHIC

SOPHIE CLAIRE

FREE BONUS:
10 FASHION TIPS EVERY STYLISH WOMAN SHOULD KNOW

Discover the 10 best fashion tips every stylish woman should know and start applying them in your own life.

Go to **www.eepurl.com/cRcn7j** to download the free guide

INTRODUCTION

Congratulations on downloading your personal copy of *French Chic: A French Woman's Guide to Dress Elegantly and Live Effortlessly Chic*. Thank you for doing so.

When it comes to style and elegance, it is a truth universally acknowledged that the French have always been a perennial figure in the world of fashion. They know it, and everyone knows that he or she can do it better.

The French do almost everything better- their food, their drinks, their culture and undeniably their fashion. Do you find yourself looking at Parisian It girls like Lou Doillon or Clemence Poesy and think, how do they look so effortless and perfect all the time and having the 'out-of-bed' hair look down to a pat, again, ever so effortlessly?

Well, you are not alone in your reverie. Because of the infatuation the entire world has on French couture and fashion, style rules on how to imitate the look began to be drawn up.

The French invest in a few key style elements- these elements serve a wardrobe for years and never run out of style. From a perfectly fitted LBD to a well-tailored jacket- investing in a few luxury yet classic items will ultimately bring you value over time.

Despite the many haute couture brands available in Paris, the French women also hold their own personal and unique style because the second rule of dressing well is to feel good in what you wear and own it.

To truly breathe and live the essence of French chic, you have to be connected with French style icons and thanks to the internet and social media you can do that, even more, closer than just by flipping through pages of a magazine.

Whether in books or TV (think Gossip Girl), in movies (remember Devil Wears Prada) or social media, Paris Fashion Weeks forms an integral part of the fashion world. To be invited to sit in any shows during the PFW, or walk the runways for any of the shows- that means you've made it.

There is truth to this statement- the last stop for fashion month is Paris Fashion Week, and it is by far the most fashionable and the most watched fashion shows. After NYFW, London and Milan, the big guns of the fashion world from Lanvin, Celine, Dior, Givenchy, Gucci and Chanel showcase their collections and set the trends for the coming year.

With big names coming from France, it is no wonder that French women have a covetable and indefinable sense of style. The French have that inane ability to look extremely chic while looking like they don't care and did not lift a finger to dress up.

French influencers like Lou Doillon and Caroline de Maigret brought in the no-makeup makeup look whereas Brigitte Bardot and Capucine brought the minimal look. Ines de la Fressange and Emannuelle Alt popularized the fitted blazer, skinny scarf and jeans look, giving it a fresh and updated look. This may sound cliché, but all trendsetters set trends instead of following trends. They have a signature look, and they stick with it.

Whether it is a black suit or a chic hobo look, the chic French style is as enviable no matter what the trends are. Not only do those who have mastered this look know what is best for your body type, but they also display an air of confidence while carrying the look.

FRENCH CHIC

CHAPTER 1:
WHAT DOES "FRENCH CHIC" MEAN?

You probably have a good idea what French chic fashion is, but do you know what it means to be 'French chic'? In the Oxford English Dictionary, the word 'chic' simply means elegance and stylishness and goes on to add 'typically of a specified kind.'
No matter the definition in the dictionary, magazines such as Harpers Bazaar and Vogue have been using this word to rain praise on designers such as Balenciaga, Chanel and Yves Saint Laurent.

The word chic has become so saturated that even Wikipedia has a list of notable chics.

Here is a timeline to go through the various meanings of what it means to be French chic right from the 17th century till today:

- 1600- As expected, the word chic as we know it today is derived from the old French word of 'chicanery' and is defined as 'sophistry and legal quibbling.' Chic is also linked to the word 'shick' in German which means skill or tact.
- 1846- Charles Baudelaire, a French critic, wrote his views on the word 'chic' saying that it is a strange and horrendous word and that even he does not know how to spell it.
- 1856- In the novel 'Madame Bovary' authored by Gustave Flaubert, the word 'chichard' is used by one of the characters to describe a stylish and everything but a bourgeois.
- 1860- Around this time, the Oxford Dictionary claims that the word chic began being used in the English Language. The variation of chic, 'chicly' also surfaced at this point.
- 1887- The word chic has been used on ladies who lunch and on January 20th in 'The Lady' edition, England's oldest weekly magazine stated in an article 'the women of New York think no

form of entertainment so chic as a luncheon party". The Lady is still in production until this day, albeit with far more different articles and causes.

- 1925- The golden age of Jazz in America also brought in the rage of chic fashion. In Anita Loo's book, Gentlemen Prefer Blondes, the story follows Lorelei Lee, a blonde, as she goes about documenting her life in a diary-style way, complete with spelling mistakes and grammatical errors. In the book, which was first published in Harper's Bazaar, Lorelei uses the word 'sheik' to describe just about anything.
- 1938- In the 1938 issue of Harper's Bazaar, an article reports Cristobal Balenciaga's talent by mentioning how the designer abides by one of the fashion's rules of less is more and says that it is chic.

- 1944- The Firebrand of Florence, a short-lived Broadway show has a character singing 'my weakness is chic-ness.'
- 1954- Fashion goddess Audrey Hepburn was the ultimate chic woman. Mention chic and this Hollywood prima donna comes to mind. Thanks to Edith Head, stylist of Hollywood's Golden Age, Hepburn was the darling in the limelight and a style icon that won multiple Oscars. In the movie Sabrina, Hepburn wore one of Head's dresses. Head claims that if anyone without chic wore it, it would never have become a style.
- 1965- At this time, the word chic become more and more prominent, and other subsets of the word started to take shape. You can start seeing words like 'tres chic' and 'uber-chic,' a German-inspired takeaway. Magazines were also talking about 'super-chic.'
- 1966- Yves Saint Laurent brings chic back into French chic by redefining what it means to be French chic in a Le Smoking tuxedo suit. The suit embodies minimalist styles for women and thus, solidifying the androgyny look.
- 1968- French chic takes a whole new refreshed wave with famous trendsetters such as Brigitte Bardot, Ines de la Fressange, Catherine Deneuve and Jane Birkin, thus ushering a new era of devil-may-care attitude and redefining chic.
- 1976- The first ever issue of pornographic Chic Magazine is published with Larry Flynt at the helm
- 1978- Disco band chic releases a track called 'Le Freak' with a line in the song which goes "Le freak, c'est chic."
- 1993- Supermodels Naomi Campbell and Kate Moss dine what it means to be 'model chic' and thus, once again redefining a new era of chic which is also known as the 'model-off-duty' style.
- 2006- The MET pays tribute to cultural icons of chic-ness Nan Kempner with the exhibition called 'American Chic.'

- 2010-. Boho-chic takes on a whole new meaning with the popularity of the fashion twins Mary-Kate and Ashley Olsen encompassing layers of coats and baggy pants with lived-in hair. Their evolution goes on to represent more understated chic with The Row, their luxury ready-to-wear line.
- 2011- Fall 2011 sees the designs of Peter Copping for Nina Ricci with the goal to redefine chic again.
- 2014- Another subset of chic is defined in Geek Chic which came out in the late 90s and stayed on, featuring an infusion of fashion and technology. Chic-ness becomes more relevant than ever especially since this geek chic is in its own level of sophistication and elegance. Models can be seen rocking Google Glass, and Apple watched down the runway.
- 2015- Chic goes back to its French roots which an all-new wave of fashion influencers in the likes of Carine Roitfeld and Marion Cotillard, Audrey Tatou and Eva Green.

As you can see from this timeline, what it means to be chic is defined over and over again because fashion is an evolution. Designers and It girls are always out there to break the glass ceiling and continue to redefine rules and essentials of clothing. There are not set-in-stone rules. Depending on what is popular, what trends people seek out and who is wearing what, fashion rules concerning chic-ness is undeniably a trend that many women want to master.

Even now, come 2017, it is also chic to be eco-friendly.

However, when it comes to French chic, it is always something people relate to being classic, elegant and sophistication without trying too hard.

SOPHIE CLAIRE

CHAPTER 2:
FRENCH FASHION INFLUENCERS

A big part of following a particular trend, especially as something everlasting as French chic is to follow the trendsetters or influencers of the style. Plenty of notable icons created their own sense of style while at the same time mixing and matching with current trends. If you want to follow the French chic movement, then you need to know who your fashion idols are and what kind of chic-ness do they bring to the table.

• Betty Catroux

This woman is a legend and very much sought after by fashion designers who look for real women who have the ability to display the indefinable French indifference. This leggy and waiflike woman has become, till this day, Tom Ford's muse and inspiration. Back in the heyday of the 60s and 70s, Betty was a booked model for Yves Saint Laurent and Chanel though it was the former that made her the face of YSL. Betty is known for her strong personality and many associate her French chic with the androgynous look.

• Bettina

In the 1940s and 1950s, Bettina was a force to reckon with and a powerhouse that established Paris as the capital of the fashion world. A French model and muse to couturier Jacques Fath, Bettina had dramatic custom-made couture and set as well as impeccable and avant-garde hats that were synonymous with her style and a staple that she wore to events and parties.

Bettina in her heyday was the epitome of French chic icon. Known also as the first supermodel in France, Bettina gained immense popularity for shoots done with famous photographers such as Irving Penn.

• Brigitte Bardot

Highly doubt anyone not living under a rock will be able to forget the name, Brigitte Bardot. Even if you were born a millennial, you would eventually encounter her famous name. Brigitte Bardot is amongst the most well-known French sex symbols thanks to her scandalous roles in movies such as Le Mepris as well as "And God Created Women'. Brigitte had a different persona both on and off screen. On-screen, you would see her with coquettish bows at one point and also in black leather. But off-screen, Brigitte pulls of classic ballet flats, chic off-shoulder tops as well as beautiful summery dresses.

• Capucine

Capucine, despite not being as famous as other French models and actresses of her time, she is known for a signature style when it comes to French chic. Capucine can be seen in staples that define her sense of chic by wearing turbans, elbow-length gloves, chunky pearl earrings and elegant suits. These various combinations sometimes made her look ladylike and sometimes edgy. Thanks to her movie role in 'The Pink Panther,' Capucine became a household name, instantly recognizable as the funny and chic girl. Her modeling also took off following her role in the movie, and she walked for the likes of Givenchy and Christian Dior.

• Carine Roitfeld

To be a Vogue Editor is one of the most coveted titles in the publishing world and that is what Carine is notable for, as the former editor of Vogue Paris. Over the many years as the editor, Carine has a unique style that is so French chic. Her wardrobe choices range from the neutral colors of grays, blacks, navy blues, browns as well as cream. There is rarely a time where you would find her in a color palette that is white. Carine prefers her fashion to be classic with unexpected twists here and there such as a sheet skirt, an elegant peek of skin, and she also loves a smoky eye. Balmain and Givenchy are among her favorite go-to designers.

• Coco Chanel

This list of influencers would not be complete without Coco Chanel in it. Very few fashion designers especially back in the day are known as style icons as they are fashion designers. Coco Chanel is among them who do double duty. Coco Chanel designs her clothes based on what she would wear not what other women would wear. She was her first customer and her best critic. Her fashion choices created trends that women felt at ease in but at the same time, chic. Her staples include layered costume jewelry, knits, and jerseys as well as the ever-present little black dress.

• Francoise Hardy

French bohemian chic was created by Hardy in the late 60s. Despite that, her fashion choices are still trendy and modern in today's world as it was 60 years ago. Francoise favored sleek Courreges pantsuits as well as Paco Rabanne chainmail dresses. She also has a liking for little white dresses, white books, chunky furs as well as knitted dresses and chic-fringe attires.

• Ines de la Fressange

This iconic businesswoman, fashion designer, and French model prefer classic pieces from skinny scarves to fitted blazers, denim jackets and layers of pearl necklaces to create texture and elevate minimal and basic pieces. You would often see de la Fressange in more comfortable clothing such as loose pants with a well fitted top rather than fancy skirts and fussy dresses. The red carpet or fashion shows are no different. This is what makes Ines de la Fressange quintessentially French chic.

• Jacqueline de Ribes

Jacqueline is known for many things but a boring woman she is not. One of the most photographed aristocrats of French upper class, Jacqueline is also a fierce businesswoman, couture collector and style icon that is so prolific till an entire exhibition was conducted to showcase her personal wardrobe at the Met. Jacqueline is also a prominent figure on the global party circuit especially since Paris; her birthplace is the city of lights and love. Her motto in life is to live life in excess and to have everything custom made if she can have her way.

• Sonia Rykiel

Sonia is a woman who created and established her look. With her blazing trademark red hair, Sonia is often seen wearing knits which are also featured in her many pieces as a designer. Sonia is always out to make statement pieces and was one of the first few designers to expose seams and use words on clothing and soft sweaters.

• Victoire de Castellane

Victoire is a French creative director and jewelry designer for Christian Dior's line of elegant and exquisite jewelry. She brings in her robust and bold sense of chic that can be seen in the colors as well as the shape and imagination that exudes from her wardrobe and inspires her jewelry designs.

From teddy bear shaped handbags to wild accessories, book clutches and textured and patterned silhouettes, Sonia can bring anything to life whether

19

it is a boxy bomber jacket or a shimmery red dress.

• Clemence Poesy

Clemence is a maverick at mixing Parisian chic with Brooklyn hippy vibes. This French actress and fashion model are popular for her movie roles in American cinema. Starred in the likes of Gossip Girl, Poesy off-red carpet look embodies Parisian insouciance with staples such as oxford shoes, embroidered sweaters, and comfy jeans.

• Anna Karina

Anna became popular through her starring roles in French New Wave films from prominent directors such as Jean-Luc Godard. Though Danish-born, Anna has a chic and retro style about her and can be seen in sweaters with bold fringes, primary-hued jackets, skillfully applied cat eyeliner and little dresses equipped with Peter Pan collars. Anna is known for a witty and sardonic French attitude, complete with cigarette in hand.

All these icons described are classic icons that started, crystallized and made the chic French fashion that we know of today. Without their boldness and braveness to reinvent fashion and to define how a woman should dress, the fashion world as we know it today would not be the same.

Google images of them and pin it to your Pinterest fashion boards to get inspired whenever you plan your next fashion shopping spree. Since most of the clothing items are essential wardrobe items, you are guaranteed to find something similar or close to what these icons have worn in magazine spreads, covers, their films and in advertisements.

CHAPTER 3:
PARISIAN INSTAGRAM INFLUENCERS TO FOLLOW FOR MAJOR INSPIRATION

At this day and age, flipping through fashion magazines or TV channels aren't the only place for inspiration. Instagram is a haven for all things inspiration whether fashion, food, technology, art, music, exercise, fitness, and sports. To these Instagrammers, Paris Fashion Week isn't just a show of beautiful clothes and trends with after parties. It is a way of life and following these accounts; you bet yourself you can find anything between chic, effortless, cool, and dramatic and avant-garde.

- @carolinedemaigret

Caroline, with such a quintessentially French name, is a model and music producer by day. She is also the co-author of 'How to be Parisian Wherever You Are' written especially for women looking to embody the Parisian chic no matter where in the world they are. On her gram, you will see a unique selection of menswear with that oh-so-French subtle sex appeal peaking through. She also accompanies her photos with wit and humor, often coming across as kooky which is why she has 651k followers and counting. They can relate to her kookiness and her style.

- @jeannedamas

Jeanne is your girl-next-door who has acquired some of the chicest items you can find. On her account, you can find minute details of what it takes to dress like a true Parisian as well as bonafide pictures of her life as one of Instagram's It girls. She is cool, she is friendly, and she covers just about anything in her life, even to her amazing cats. Jeanne also runs successful fashion blogs with strict lessons for the Parisian wannabe.

- @adelinerapon

Not sure how to style your curls? Then look no further from Adeline Rapon's Instagram. Here you will see a composed and confident woman with a unique brand of French chic styling. A blogger, jeweler and amateur photographer, Adeline is constantly in collaboration with another of Paris's fashion darling, Louise Pando. Not sure how to use those beautiful berets? Learn it from Adeline (or copy, rather).

- @dennielias

Alumni of Parson's School of Art, Denni is often exploring the globe encountering one glamorous venue after another. Her photos look so high-end they seem to be snipped out from the pages of Vogue itself. Denni loves thigh high boots, and you'd think it looks tacky but the way she wears it and pairs it up with oversized sweaters and beautiful day dresses, you'd be hard-pressed not to buy the next thigh high boots you see.

- @camillecharriere

A Parisian living in London, Camille did not forget to bring her Parisian style and taste. A longtime blogger in the fashion world, Camille sometimes favors boyish chic with t-shirts and ripped jeans or sometimes in girly chic with flowy floral dresses. Her Instagram often focuses on fashion mostly but also artistic photography.

- @adenorah

If you love retro fashion but want a modern and fresh version of it, then look to Adenorah for inspiration. Browsing through her Instagram, you can see high-waisted denim, oversized sunglasses, and disheveled hair and micro minis. She is the digital age, Farrah Fawcett. The modern retro take looks hard to follow, but Adenorah makes it look effortless.

- @cuillereaabsinthe

Stylish, actress and Baby DJ, Cuillere have a quirky sense of hipster chic, and you can see how she makes athleisure so comfortable and stylish. She is forever looking for ways to reinvent fashion rules and has a love for tennis shoes and sneakers.

- @slanelle

On her Instagram account, you can see Slanelle's love for Japanese fashion. Colorful, bold and bright, Slanelle takes the Harajuku sense of boldness and reinvents it with Parisian chic. These combinations are cheerful and fun and embody her tagline of traveling with color. She is also a vlogger on

YouTube, sharing tutorials from hairdos to nail art.

- @sarah_nait

Sleek and black is what you can call Sarah's Instagram account. Her photos are something out of an art exhibition celebrating a mysterious woman. She exudes a sense of mystery on her photos- you can see her but not find her. This is an excellent account for visual journaling, focusing on specific clothing items she wears like a delicate chain or a sleek belt. If you are looking for minimalist chic with some attitude, then Sarah's the influencer you should be following.

- @the_caroo

Caroline embodies the dreamy Parisian chic with her long, flowing blonde locks, beautiful flowy dresses, and sleek heels, all showcased against the backdrop of the City of Lights. She is among France's longtime fashion bloggers and bonafide Instagrammer. From summery frocks to glitter gowns, Caroline is feminine sophistication.

CHAPTER 4:
WHAT ARE THE ESSENTIALS OF FRENCH CHIC?

You may not be French, and you may not have visited France, but that doesn't stop you from enjoying their food, fashion, style, and flair.

Paying attention to what French girls wear is much easier now since we have the internet. A simple Google search or a Pinterest browse will give you image after image of what is defined as Parisian or French chic. Pinterest brings the whole searching and browsing thing to a whole new level as you can pin and make notes of what these French women wear so you can replicate it in your own wardrobe.

While the French women create their own sense of style, there are however certain rules of styling that they follow and these style rules are universal ones.

As the French say 'Bon chic, bon genre' which means *Good Style, Good Attitude*.

To dress well is to also project a good attitude.

Also, Bon Chic Bon Genre is shortened to BCBG which is how BCBG Max Azria got its name.

While not all French women dress in French chic, the ones that do however aren't often found in a classic, stylish and simple style, sometimes conservative sometimes avant-garde and sometimes radical.

But for the most part, here are the essentials that you want to equip your wardrobe with to achieve the French Chic style.

Here are the few ground rules:

1. No flashing of logos or brands

You wouldn't see any French woman carrying bags with French labels emblazoned vividly. You wouldn't even find French women with LV bags with their signature logos all around it. The French chic tend to avoid any flamboyant show of wealth.

The French women have a different experience with brand image compared to the rest of the world. While the rest of us probably prefer outward expressions of wealth and branded items, the French women seem to go with more subtle showings which are usually either a small logo or none at all.

For the women who are born and bred in France, they let their style speak for them. You would often see understated Chanel bags, held discreetly or the eponymous Burberry trench coat with logo shown. The idea is that just by looking at the item of clothing, one can tell if it is an expensive brand or not without looking at a logo as the French chic woman carries it with class. For those that follow fashion trends and the latest collections, they can spot if that specific coat is a Burberry coat or a Birkin bag.

2. Neutrals are a key color palette

Colors are one of those things that are a personal preference for the French chic woman. Some wear bold colors while most stick with neutral colors. These bold colors are usually in the form of statement jewelry or a skinny scarf, in shoes, bags and other accessories.

Ivory, white, beige and burgundy are favorite color palettes for the French chic and usually black, grey, navy and brown are usual players in a French woman's wardrobe.

Parisian women tend to not wear a lot of colors. That is, barely any. If they do wear it, it's in accessories like their scarves, jewelry, shoes, bags.. you know stuff like that.

Black, plays a major role in the Parisian chic wardrobe as they give that classic taste to any fashion piece.

When it comes to makeup, French women also like bold lips and is usually since in a variety of red hues.

3. They follow a certain uniform of sorts

The French women technically mastered the idea of capsule wardrobes long before anyone else did. There is a basic French chic uniform that you would most often find it French woman who embodies the chic sense of style albeit putting their own unique take on it.

In the wardrobe of the French chic fashionista, you would often find skinny jeans and ballet flats, good sleek stilettos, a fitting t-shirt and blazer and also a well fitting leather jacket.

4. Over accessorizing is a big no-no

As the greatest fashion icon, Coco Chanel said 'Before you leave the house, look in the mirror and remove one accessory.'

While accessories create texture, over-accessorizing, on the other hand, can kill an outfit. The French chic woman has abided to this fashion rule by the great Coco Chanel and always looks put together whether it's a chunky necklace they're wearing or a statement bangle or a huge hoop earring.

5. They save the sky-high heels for the red carpet

Or gala dinner. Many French women are rarely seen with towering, sky-high platform heels in order to be sexy. They exude sexiness very subtly without any excessive display or skin or stripper heels.

When wanting to be French chic, Kim Kardashian is your last icon to follow. Tacky heels do not spell sexy, and no French woman would be caught dead in something that she isn't comfortable in.

This goes to say that the French chic do not wear heels. They do but not the stripper kind. You'd most often see them in ballet flats, short boots, three to 4-inch heels and tall boots.

6. They never look uncomfortable

You'd never see the French chic looking uncomfortable in the clothes they wear. The women wear classic pieces that make them comfortable and make them look good. You wouldn't see them in tight-fitting dresses that restrict airflow and neither would you see them in clothing too short or too low. The women that follow the French chic idealism where sexy clothing that is well fitted; accentuating their greatest assets is a tasteful and graceful way.

Nothing is less sexy than a woman that is trying too hard to be sexy because she will look uncomfortable. Sometimes wearing the most basic items can be sexy when you feel confident and comfortable in them.

7. Always dress up rather than dress down

That being said, they may not be rocking heels and black dress every day, but you wouldn't catch French chic woman dressing up like a basic girl with Ugg boots and a sweat suit when they leave the house.

Looking presentable is the goal without looking so over the top. You want to impress but not look as if took hours to decide on what to wear. The point is, French women, dress up wanting to look presentable and casual because you never know who you'd meet!

There are clothes that they wear at home, and there are clothes that they wear exclusively outside the house. There is no 'day off' for the French woman even if she wants to run off to the store. No going out with pajamas rather, she will wear real pants and shoes.

8. The French makeup

When it comes to makeup, the French chic makeup usually focuses on one bold item. It's either a good eye makeup with a neutral lip or a bold red lip with neutral eyes or on most days, a well-lined eye with soft blush and nude lips. The French chic makeup is not a heavily made-up look. It is a subtle mix of the bold and the minimal.

Sometimes there is an extremely minimal makeup, such as a lip gloss with lightly brushed mascara and a soft dab of blush. Lipstick and mascara seem to be the most commonly worn items by the French women and they, like the Koreans, do not cover up their skin to airbrushed perfection.

The average French chic women want dewy and moisturized skin compared to cake on makeup with obvious contouring of the skin.

Now that we have covered the basic essentials and style guidelines of what it means to be French chic, here are some outfit choices that you can try your hands with:

Outfit choices of the average Parisian Chic woman:

• The Casually Polished Look Outfit

The casual polished look usually encompasses neutral colors from the beige to the nude. Sometimes it can be totally black, but more often you'd see the Parisian woman with a simple and crisp white dinner jacket with a statement tee underneath for a pop of color. Often this look is paired with nude ballet flats and aviators and skinny jeans. A scarf is usually in a bold color if not the crossbody bag.

• The *Working Chic* Outfit

The working chic outfit usually has black in it and sometimes, one hundred percent black from the head to the toes. Three-inch mary janes completed the skirt and sweater look, with a black clutch tucked underneath her arm, and a pair of sunglasses gave off a mysterious look about her. The one thing that popped was her gorgeous red lip that was a bold statement, together with a pair of simple pearl stud earrings.

This look is minimal, yet the different textures pull the entire outfit together without looking too prim and proper. The working chic outfit can also have a leather jacket either in tan or black that made this otherwise conservative look a little toughened up. Hair can be swept into a simple ponytail.

- The *Mother of Three* outfit

Forget about those stereotype mom images you often see in commercials that are usually filled with moms in button-up shirts and three-quarter pants. The Parisian chic mother has her hair either loosely plaited in a braid or in a messy bun with deep red lips, light touch of mascara that gives off an effortless and comfortable look. This simple look is easy to pull together when you are a mother of three young children because it is really effortless. You can pair up comfortable white jeans with an off shoulder tee and a slight silver chain running down for an elongated look.

- The *Coffee with your Friends* outfit

Another pulled-together black outfit except the touch of color came from her bright accessories and her scarf. Again, this ensemble while minimal looks extremely comfortable yet very stylish. This look can be very liberating and paired with well-fitted biker boots, you can have coffee and head to a bar when night falls.

Conclusion

Now that we have an idea of the French chic mindset and we have a few examples of the kinds of outfit that can be worn, here is a concluded list of wardrobe essentials that you can acquire in order to dress chic the way the French do. These items work well for any seasons but certain pieces here, and there should be added to your wardrobe in order to showcase your own personal style.

Of course, depending on what the weather's like where you live, you may also want to add in some winter boots as well as a good winter jacket to your wardrobe. Otherwise, this list covers most of the basics that you need for the entire year.

The Ideal French Chic Wardrobe:

BLAZERS / JACKETS / TOPPERS

- White blazer — A tuxedo or dinner-style jacket
- Black blazer — always an essential in any wardrobe you create
- Black leather jacket — how about making this brown or tan rather than black?
- Mixed tweed/leather jacket —this jacket makes up for a dressy and also a casual look depending on how you style them.

SWEATERS

- Navy sweater — A must in any wardrobe
- Camel sweater — Another essential item in a neutral tone
- Black turtleneck — preferably cowled or thick neck or in thin knit.

SHIRTS / TOPS

- Fitted black t-shirt — Always never go wrong
- Fitted white t-shirt — Must have always
- White drapey t-shirt — A loose t-shirt in grey, navy or black or any other neutral color works wonders
- Navy patterned tank top
- Graphic grey tank top — for casual pairings with jeans and other pants
- Plain grey tank top
- Striped Navy blue long-sleeved shirt
- White long-sleeved shirt

PANTS

- Black skinny jeans
- Dark denim jeans — either in boot-cut or skinny or even straight legged
- Black trousers — a classy, thin trouser

SKIRTS

- Black pencil skirt – well-fitted absolute must have
- Flared black skirt — To add another layer of texture and dimension

DRESSES

- Casual grey summer dress in a pinstripe
- Black sheath dress
- Bold summer dress

COAT

- Autumn or Winter wool coat in a neutral color

SHOES / HEELS / BOOTS

- Leather sandals
- Ballet flats
- Black pumps —in a chic, classy, manageable height
- Tall leather boots
- Short biker boots

PURSES

- Black clutch
- Casual satchel bag
- Structured bag

ACCESSORIES

- Simple minimalist watch
- Sunglasses
- Gloves
- Circle scarf
- A fun patterned scarf
- A bright scarf
- Pearl studs
- Dangly earrings
- Delicate necklace with a small pendant
- Layered chain necklaces (in gold and silver)

Et voilà! With these essentials, you can mix and match to your heart's desire and you would have plenty of outfit choices for the entire year whether it is winter or spring, summer or autumn. Just remember to keep it simple, adding a pop of color either in your makeup or accessories.

CHAPTER 5:
WHAT ARE THE PRINCIPLES
OF FRENCH STYLE?

As we can conclude by now, French chic is having that effortless and minimalistic sense of flair and style. Depending on who wears them and they personality, there are many variations of French chic, but there are common traits that carry in each version.

These traits boil down to two important aspects:

1. Putting thought into what matches well and what clothing items complement each other
2. But at the same time making it seem so effortless like you didn't put much thought into it and just put on whatever that you found in your closet.

Get it?

A scene that best describes this moment can be seen in Gossip Girl and the character differences between Blair and Serena.

There is one scene where Serena gets dressed for school and literally just puts on whatever that she can find while rummaging through her penthouse suite in the hotel and picking up her school tie and tying up her hair.

By contrast, Blair looks prim and proper and polished. It looks like she woke up early to decide what goes well with her headband, what colors to wear and what shoes to walk in.

While you can say that Blair looks chic, however, effortless is hardly a word you would use to describe her fashion style.

The idea here is to look effortless like you were born to it.

Ines de la Fressange describes in her style book, *Parisian Chic* that French chic styling is all about the basics.

- **Essential 1-Buying items that go well with anything**

When purchasing something, for the French, the big picture is important. They are not likely to buy just one piece of clothing because it looks great. Before buying an item, the French women especially are known to think about how this individual piece complements the items that are already in their existing wardrobe.

It is essential to them that each item that they purchase works to create a complete and effortless outfit. This is a rule that almost everyone with a sense of style has mastered. Great style isn't about having a closet full of Manolos or Birkins or LVs but how you skillfully put one basic piece with another statement piece to create a chic look.

They prefer how an entire look comes together rather than buying individual items that do not look good with other pieces.

- **Essential 2- Matching and coordinating are two different things**

When we think about fashion and the elites of the fashion world, you will notice that none of them walk out of the house looking matchy in head-to-toe red or leopard prints or garish floral ensembles.

Parisian chic is about balance and the need to coordinate rather than to match. If it is a floral dress, then they might offset it with a plain leather jacket.

If something is sporty, then she might add something feminine either in color or in terms of accessory.

It is all about striking a balance without having too much of something. If you are still confused with this whole notion, just remember that it about needing to coordinate your outfit, looking slightly rough around the edges but put together at the same time.

- **Essential 3- Getting your color palette right**

A big part of the eclectic Parisian woman is the fact that she loves breaking fashion rules and creating styles that suit her needs and personality. But the big difference between her and the rest of us is that she knows what rules to follow and which to break. Among them are the choices of color and its importance in putting together a well coordinated yet effortless outfit.

Instead of navy blue jeans, she will probably use white jeans and pair it with a black turtleneck and reach for her tan leather jacket instead of her skinny navy sweater. It's about wearing a chunky necklace or a pair of statement earrings and not both. She sticks to the basics and what her body is comfortable in but also experiments here and there with different styles and hues.

- **Essential 4- The Androgyny look**

Fashion is not something that exists in dresses only. Fashion is in the sky, in the street, fashion has to do with ideas, the way we live, what is happening.

- *Coco Chanel*

Thanks to Coco Chanel, the androgyny look is something all women deign to look, but only a few have mastered. Chanel wanted women to wear clothes that did not exaggerate her femininity with frills and flounces at every shop window and boutique. She designed clothing that had straight lines, clean shapes and simple silhouettes and that is how the androgyny look came to be and stayed.

Chanel was a true blue Parisian who could take any plain and ordinary looking garment and make it into her own personal style, and just like Coco Chanel, all other Parisian women maintain this balance of exuding their femininity together with looks and styles with the masculine fashion.

An equilibrium is achieved where gender lines are blurred.

- **Essential 5- The basics should still be your staple**

"The little black dress is not simply an item of clothing, it's a concept. It's abstract, it's universal — which means there's one that's perfect for everyone ... Today the Parisian has several little black dresses, just as she has several pairs of jeans: each is a variation on a theme."

~Inès de la Fressange

Wardrobe basics are an essential part of life and yes life because these basics need to be in anyone's wardrobe or cupboard or closet because they are staples. These staples are:

- A white shirt
- A striped t-shirt

- A plain white t-shirt
- Black pants
- Dark jeans
- Nude shoes
- Classic black flats
- Structured leather bag
- Strappy stilettos
- Little Black/White Dress
- A blazer
- Good underclothing

The French chic wardrobe has all these essentials and a little bit more, which is why they always look put-together. It isn't about owning a lot of clothing items or the most expensive, but it is owning the classic items that work with just about anything and can be paired and matched to created plenty of different looks.

These basics are the difference between someone who feels like they have nothing to wear compared to someone who always has pieces to wear for an easy to pull off look. Stocking up on versions or variations of a basic essential such as plain t-shirts in various colors or statement jewelry can really elevate any look. Instead of only having one dark skinny denim pants, a variation could be blue straight cut jeans.

Sequined ballet flats are a great variation to the classic black. The options are endless if you know what the staples are and how to vary them. The French idea of fashion understands the importance of basics, and that transcends to life as well. Fashion isn't about spending your entire time picking out what to wear because real women have better things to do with their time. Even if you are someone who isn't a trendy person or follows fashion trends or even understand fashion, investing in the basics will help you put on a great ensemble together.

- **Essential 6- Always good to dress up and never down**

Here is why having the basics in your wardrobe helps you dress up even when you just want to dress down. Sure there are days when you just feel like throwing on whatever that you can reach before heading out the door but when you have the basics in your closet, a simple plain black t-shirt paired with skinny blue jeans, short boots, and a crossbody will help you look chic and comfortable even when the weather is freezing out there. Put on your comfortable coat, and you are out of the house.

The French understand the importance of uplifting yourself through fashion and dressing better epitomizes this concept. This also helps in making sure you do not waste and also helps you financially.

Buying the basics helps you pair more things together instead of having a separate stash of ugly ill-fitting clothes that you don't feel like trying at all.

Comfort is key in the Parisian chic. The women may look like they spend hours and hours in front of the mirror getting every inch of hair right, but essentially, while they do take their time, they use it wisely in determining what to wear and what items go well and make quick decisions about it. While comfort is crucial, achieving comfort and looking good is what makes you chic.

- **Essential 7- Accessories! Accessories! Accessories!**

Do you remember that scene in *'The Devil Wears Prada'* where Andy stupidly laughs when the assistant tells Miranda it's hard to choose between two turquoise belts?

Miranda understands the power of accessorizing. It can definitely take a basic plain tee into a stylish tee in a matter of seconds. French fashion is about dressing like you want to conquer the world, hence spending time wisely is essential. That said, accessories are also part of the basic essentials such as a pair of oversized sunglasses, silk scarves, and a good watch. For jewelry, it is either minimal or none at all. The French chic woman sticks to gold or silver toned jewelry, pearls, and chunky statement necklaces or a thin chain necklace.Shoes are often pointed heels or riding boots, flats, sandals, and pumps are stylish yet comfortable. There is no room for flip-flops, heavy boots, and trainers.

- **Essential 8- Own your look**

Part of being chic is also about not being pretentious and having no real talk. The French also pride themselves in their homegrown French labels. They are also about owning who they are, their minds, bodies, flaws and anything they love because it makes them who they are. The central of French fashion is having a strong sense of personal style as well as being genuine.

This is why the French treat fashion as art and just like all art forms, the classic rules must be learnt and mastered before attempting anything above and beyond. Fashion like art is a form of self-expression.

CHAPTER 6:
THE ESSENTIALS IN A
FRENCH CHIC CAPSULE WARDROBE

In this chapter, we will look at 14 essential style guides that are specially curated for the French-inspired Capsule Wardrobe! Capsule wardrobes are great because it starts off with the basics and the French are all about the basics.

If you'd like a more in-depth guide of the capsule wardrobe I suggest you to check out my book *Capsule Wardrobe: Discover Your Personal Style And Create Your Dream Wardrobe*, available at Amazon.

Starting out with a French capsule wardrobe is ideally one of the best ways to being your journey into becoming a woman who embodies the Parisian way of dressing- effortless yet stylish.

Drawing inspiration from fashion icons like Ines de La Fressange, Jane Birkin, Marion Cotillard and Audrey Tatou to name a few, these 14 essential pieces help you hone your inner French girl. Each of this essential item captures the essence of chic French women of the modern world so that it will be a lot easier for you to emulate their styles and purchase clothing items that are similar to the ones described here.

Whether it is the simple sheath dresses of Carla Bruni or Marion Cottilard's plain shirts to Ines's skinny cigarette pants and Lou Dillion's chic tank tops- these essentials exemplify each of this beautiful women's personification of French chic.

These modern women are an extension of the classics of French style, the founding sisterhood of French chic such as Coco Chanel, Brigitte Bardot, and Catherine Deneuve. No matter, where you look in the streets of Paris or the glistening shops of the French boulevards, you would see these women walking down incorporating at least one of these essentials on them.

1. Get yourself a handbag

Lets' face it. A woman cannot have only one bag. Capsule wardrobes are just that- capsule, small and only for needed items. So how do you fit bags into a capsule wardrobe?

You pick a bag that is versatile. This bag needs to be good quality, and it needs to be versatile as a work bag and a day bag. Ideally, a small cross-body bag would also help for those weekends out.

Find a bag that fits your budget. Remember, it isn't using branded items that make you chic rather how you carry these items and how it complements your entire look that matters.

Your bag should fit your budget and ultimately your lifestyle, and it also needs to last. These three factors are important when choosing a bag for your capsule wardrobe.

2. Ankle skimming jeans and pants

Purchasing a well-tailored cigarette, skinny or straight leg skinny jeans and pants is one of the best assets of your wardrobe – be it capsule or not. These essentials can be paired with anything. It is also worth noting that when investing in these pants, you also want it to be versatile enough to be used for many different seasons. Straight legged jeans are a perennial staple, and so is the cigarette cut. Depending on your body shape, you might want to choose pants that has an opening that flatters your shape- either making you curvier or making you slimmer or taller. Either choice that you make on your pants ensure that the hem goes right up to the top of your ankle. Capris or culottes are not part of the wardrobe trend we want to stock up on because they tend to cut the length of the leg and disrupt the slimming effect.

3. Flats

If flats aren't part of your wardrobe- get them now! Flats are so versatile, and while stilettos and high heels make you look amazing, they cannot be worn with every outfit especially if walking is part of your daily routine.

The French women favor kitten heels and ballet flats for everyday walking compared to sky-high stilettos you often see American women walking down in Wall Street. And because of the French chic look so effortless with ballet flats, everyone else wants in on this trend. A pair of black and nude flats needs to be a must-have component in your wardrobe- pronto!

4. The black dress

Need we say more? You know it is versatile. You know it can be used for work with a simple blazer. You know it can be utilized for a night out without the blazer. It is fuss free, versatile and chic.

5. The Blazer

Speaking of blazers, this is another essential item in your capsule wardrobe. The color depends on what your personal preference is but essentially, navy blue, black, taupe and white is a preferred choice as they can be paired easily with everything in your capsule wardrobe. One thing to take note off is that bad tailoring will destroy a blazer so make sure that you get a tailored blazer that fits your body frame. Once you have this, you can pair it up with your skinny jeans, cigarette pants and even your black dress. Versatility is the power of the blazer.

6. Scarves

Purchasing scarves depend on the weather and climate that you live in. But then again, scarves are as versatile as blazers and can be worn with just about anything. It is also easier to shop for one and when there is no appropriate accessory in sight, grab a scarf, and you are good to go. Scarves remind me of how Elle Woods (Legally Blonde) turned her black lawyer outfit to a fashionable one with just a simple scarf around her neck. For cooler months, a cozy cashmere scarf does the trick whereas, for spring and summer, lightweight printed scarves are ideal.

Scarves compliment a capsule wardrobe because they do not need much storage space and you don't need to spend a fortune on them (unless you're buying Hermes).

7. Sunglasses

Oversized sunglasses may not be an essential item, but hey, it keeps out the glaring sunlight from our eyes and is also frames your face and elevates an outfit. Aviator sunglasses are the ideal statement piece for any face shape.

8. An expensive t-shirt

Are you ready to spend that kind of money? Well simply put, an expensive shirt layered with a good blazer creates that effortlessly chic look. While we are all out for purchasing t-shirts for leisure at bargain prices, a good and expensive t-shirt creates an avant-garde look to an otherwise casual outfit. A good selection would be a t-shirt that is a combination of jersey and cotton so that it has a little stretch. This look gives your effortless, it gives you comfort, and it also gives you cool without trying too hard.

9. The oversized sweater

Blasé aloofness is perfected with the oversized blouse, coat or sweater. As a matter of fact, it isn't only the French women donning this look. It is such a favorite that many countries all around the world have something similar to an oversized sweater. But don't pair your oversized top with an oversized bottom. Remember that being chic is also having restraint and if you are wearing an oversized sweater than your bottom should be shorts, a good skirt or a pair of tailored pants. Balancing these two opposites is what being chic is all about.

10. Trenchcoat

Trench coats are ideal for colder climates so if you live in warmer climates; you can make do without this. Trench coats in khaki, print, or black offer your wardrobe a timeless silhouette. Essentially, the classic trench is a mid-length one in taupe, gray, navy or black is ideal for the effortlessly chic look.

11. White button-up shirt

Just like the little black dress, the white button-down shirt is a staple. When you do not know what to wear, reach out for your white shirt, ballet flats and jeans. Tuck in or tuck out the shirt and add either a simple necklace or a statement piece, carry a clutch in your hand, and you are ready to go. This look is simple, it is appropriate, and it is comfortable. A crisp white shirt can never go wrong. Just like the blazer, make sure your shirt is also well tailored and fits well on you.

12. The day dress

Dress, in one motion, gets us women dressed up and with one or two accessories; we are ready to paint the town red. Having a dress that flatters our frame and makes us feel good is priceless. Your day dress can be a shirt dress or an A-Line dress or a wrap or sheaths, good dresses are timeless and something that can be worn for every season. Just make sure this day dress follows your sense of style and the Parisian chic you want to embody.

13. Stripes

Whenever you think of the French or to be more accurate, French styling and French related cultural items often come in stripes. Mime artist- he wears stripes! French It girl? She is known wearing stripes. Call it a stereotype, but it was Coco Chanel's momentous decision that has made stripes the iconic symbol of French chic fashion. Use stripes for your tops and blouses but never for your pants or skirts.

14. Black everything

Part of the chic wardrobe is an endless supply of black clothing items because black is a forever piece. Layer it, wear it, add a pop of statement pieces and it takes the B out of boring. Anything with black is tres chic.

Conclusion

Capsule wardrobes are the ideal setting for engaging and immersing yourself in a French chic style and fashion. Once you have the basics understood, you can then expand a little bit more on accessories, on different types of clothing and colors to make your capsule wardrobe much more versatile. But first, learn the rules and then diversify.

CHAPTER 7:
ESSENTIALS OF
FRENCH CHIC MAKEUP

At sunny sidewalk cafes in Paris and the runways of Paris fashion week, you would have seen plenty of women in mussed-up hair and very minimal to no make-up at all. In previous chapters we talked about how the French do minimalism- it is about the basics and the accentuating the basics. It is all about complementing and not covering.
The same thing is with makeup.

Makeup is also a very personal and culturally intertwined thing. Different cultures have different perceptions of what beauty is, and therefore, the makeup women wear embodies and personify these cultural aspects.

In America, the Kim Kardashian look is popular- heavily contoured face, bold lips, bold eyes and heavy coverage. In Korea, the emphasis is on dewy skin and more so the no-makeup makeup look. In Arabian culture, the eyes are the focus with thickly lined eyes with kajal.

In France, you do one of the other. It's either the bold lips or the bold eyes OR minimal makeup OR none at all. The French idea of makeup is how to look perfectly imperfect, without trying too hard?

Here is a glimpse of the French chic girl's makeup rulebook:

1. Prep but not Primp

A French woman's objective for makeup is not to hide the flaws but rather enhance natural features. So instead of covering up every blemish and scar and pimple and wrinkle, she would most likely spend her time on getting rid of the impurities on the skin by way of facial treatments, a daily routine of cleaning, toning and moisturizing and eating right. It is about getting your skin healthy as opposed to having unhealthy skin and making it even more harmful with layers and layers of makeup.

2. Moderation is key

That said, it isn't like the French women are living without the slightest bit of color. The idea of healthy skin is not about what you put on it regarding foundation and primer and concealer. It is about what you eat as well. The French, known for their cuisine is something they savor on a daily basis. Eating isn't about munching and walloping food into their gut. It is about enjoying every bite and appreciating the time and effort that went into making a meal. Less sugar and more organic food is what is regularly consumed not so much low-in-fat though.

3. Exercise

The working out trend was virtually non existent in Paris practically a decade ago, although it is fast catching on. The barre method was from France and walking, cycling, running and jogging are all activities the French do on a regular basis, and not many French women prefer the heavy muscular weight carrying fitness types that you often see in America. The food they consume already keeps them light and slim and with light exercises, it brings a healthy flush to the skin. The chic French woman does not do hardcore workouts. Although if this is something you like, go ahead and do it.

4. They do not prefer blowouts

Everyone wants Kate Middleton's brown hair, blown out to perfection but not the chic French women. While they do like texture to their hair, they prefer washing it and letting it air dry as opposed to blowing hair out day in day out. If they do need to get a blowout, it is usually a day before they need to look good.

5. Regular Salon visits

Healthy and shiny hair is preferred by all women and so do the French, so even when the hair is messy, it doesn't look damaged or oily or dry. They prefer a good haircut compared to a really good styling product. You would probably be surprised if your average French woman doesn't own a curling iron. Shoulder length or short bobs are very much the popular go-to styles in Paris.

6. Red lips are always a French favorite

French women are all about the red lips, and it has become the identity of the Parisian chic fashion. Whether it is a crimson shade or a scarlet shade or a dark ruby red, it is a French beauty favorite. They carry the red lipstick like a fashion accessory and usually with a bold lip; you wouldn't find anything else on their face. No false eyelashes, no deep bronzer, no blush and no eyeliner. You'd probably see light mascara on the eyelash, but that's it. With perfect skin and messy hair, the look of the French chic is complete. The basics of the entire outfit are elevated with a simple color of red and bold lips.

7. No contour

French women rarely or never contour. They have an inherent dislike for shading powders or creams because why do you want to change the sculpture of the face? Contouring though in existence in the 1500s in theaters and plays and stage, was always confined to the industry of fashion and never used or attempted by the common makeup enthusiast.

Now come in Kim Kardashian and the advent of Instagram, you will see many makeup artists and enthusiasts contouring till the cows come home. When Kim tweeted a picture in 2010 of her before & after contouring, it was the time many people realized that they too, with the right tools can create chiseled jawlines and high cheekbones.

But to the French woman, instead of adding darker shades of brown, they instead bring light to the cheeks and cupid's bow of the lips.

8. Subtle smoky eye

The French love smoky eyes but theirs is more of a messy one with a creamy texture compared to a hard-lined one. This messy one gives a very soft look to the entire face rather than a harsh one.

They like a little bit of dewiness and a little bit of tinted lip balm or gloss compliments the smoky eye.

Conclusion

Essentially, the French chic makeup look is nothing too complicated. It is one or two swipes of mascara with a dab of lip gloss and some blush on the cheeks, or it is a smoky eye with light touches of lip balm, or it is a full-on the red lip with light mascara and no blush.

Also, they know that beauty is really skin deep. There is no point in lathering layers of makeup when the natural skin is in bad shape. Eating right, drinking loads of water and with good sleep is what gets the skin looking fresh and supple all day long.

Who needs extreme makeup when your skin is porcelain goodness?

CHAPTER 8:
ESSENTIALS IN
FRENCH CHIC SKINCARE

For the woman born and bred in France, she is steeped in a culture of beauty, fashion and fabulous food. Beauty routines and tips for the average French woman has been something she has learned from her mother, who has learned it from her mom and it goes way back.
These secrets of skin care are something that has been passed on for centuries. Take for example Eau Thermale Avene whose expertise spans way back to 1736 and Caudalie began its natural supplements in 1993 whereas La Roche Posay began its antioxidant thermal spring water in 1905.

The best lessons in French beauty are rooted in their lifestyle starting with a great skincare routine down to using minimal makeup. Here are a few beauty secrets from the French that you can adapt in your own way:

1. Complex skin care routine

While the French women may look and dress with a devil-may-care attitude, their skincare routine is anything but effortless. Isabel Marant, fashion designer extraordinaire once said 'It's all about attitude. And it's true; I think French girls make a lot of effort pretending they are not making any effort!'

The French value great looking skin, the same way the Koreans price porcelain skin with minimal makeup. Hence, their skin care routine is a complex one. While they do not put on a lot of makeup, they make sure that their skin is properly hydrated, washed, clean, exfoliated and healthy.

2. Thermal water is a must have

While the French woman may have a complex skincare routine, they also believe in having fewer products on the face. It always starts with a facial wash followed by a light toner. Thermal water is a must-have in this skincare regime, and it is sprayed on the face and neck. A pomade is applied on the face on an alternate day basis.

At night, it is a clean face with a good moisturizer.

Facial treatments are all the rage as well, with most women going for a facial at least once a month.

3. Beauty is from the inside

Genetics is one thing, but a bigger role in the good skin would be a lifestyle choice that we make. Eating fresh fruit and vegetables are the key to obtaining a healthy glow, together with a low-sugar diet and plenty of and drinking water and a good bit of exercise.

What you consume is very important for glowing and healthy skin. Essentially no fried foods filled with bad oil and fats. No processed food either. As much as possible, eat healthy home-cooked food, and the French are masters in making simple but delicious food. Unlike us Americans with microwave food and takeaways, the French have very simplified meals such as poached fish with steamed vegetables or a vegetable and meat pie, Friseé with bacon and half boiled eggs, chicken with leeks and onion soup. Fat is not the problem and the French delight their meals with fresh cream and amazing butter.

4. A sense of mindfulness

The French approach almost anything in life with a great sense of mindfulness whether it is their food, the way they eat and even how they enjoy themselves. Indulging in facials and mani-pedis are not a routine for the average French woman. She indulges but not on a weekly basis because guess what- high maintenance is not part of the French chic movement.

5. Spas and salons

The French women are believers in spas and salons to get that natural look, and they prefer spending their time and money on these treatments rather than on makeup. Apart from making your skin look great, it also helps you relax and rejuvenate. And when you think about it, you also spend less and less time in front of the mirror getting ready for work or a night out by wearing layers of makeup every day. In the long run, you might find that wearing little makeup results in fewer skin issues.

6. Even bath time is a ritual

The French woman, as often as possible, has a ritual for baths. While quick showers are often for weekday rush, long baths and hot showers are reserved as a weekly ritual with special oils, French apothecary salts, and therapeutic herbs. This makes for better and healthier skin, removes dead skin cells and also removes toxins.

7. Back to basics for answers

The French, like the Indians from India, are big on homemade masks and beauty treatments with several recipes passed from generations. Homegrown remedies are favored instead of chemical treatments. For example, for dry skin, a mixture of one tablespoon raw honey with fresh thyme and half an avocado massaged into the skin will help bring back the skin's natural moisture.

For oily skin, one tablespoon lemon juice together with honey and thyme and put on the skin for 15 minutes will leave your skin supple and removes excess oil.

Treatments like these differ between regions depending on what is available to them outside their garden. For example, those living in Provence, lavender are abundant and are usually used in remedies. In Brittany, seaweed is a more preferred choice for remedies.

8. Water is an integral part of skin care

Drinking water for healthy skin is one thing but adding thermal water or floral or herbal water elevates a person's skin care routine to achieve that Parisian glow. Because of this, you can find plenty of thermal water brands and women use this to spray on a hydrating mist all throughout the day. Plenty of French skin care products are water-based because they are much more absorbent and helps keep makeup looking natural too.

9. Prep your base

One of the key essential to ensure long lasting and smooth makeup is to create an even base on your skin. This prevents you from using tons of foundation on your skin. The French women know this that is why even when they wear makeup, it looks like it's their natural skin. They will not be piling on liquids and cakey powders the way you see the American girls use makeup. The French ideal is to feel comfortable in your own skin so you can forego foundation and even concealer.

10. Au naturel is always preferred

Perhaps the reason why many people across the globe envy the French beauty is that the French women look natural with literally little to no makeup at all. They favor cleaning their skin so pores and veins are less visible but even when they do have them, they don't cake them with makeup. To the French women, veins, freckles, moles, wrinkles and the like are real and unique.

Occasionally, you will see the women donning a little blusher here and some bronzer there to increase the glow that is naturally present in the face. But what they do not do is transforming them to look like a different person.

11. Accentuating their best features

Fresh, supple skin is among the best features that French women continue to achieve as it is their best accessory. Apart from minimal makeup, they focus on only highlighting one aspect on their face whether it is the eyes or just the lips or maybe just the cheekbones but never everything at once.

The idea here is to make one central feature prominent and the rest just to complement that focus. Minimalism in the French isn't just limited to their clothes but to their makeup as well. It is about being sensible, and it also prevents you from looking confused. It is either you go with a dramatic cat eye or a bold lip or maybe even none. Because of this almost bare look, it creates a sort of subtle sexiness that is apparent.

12. Look effortless but polished

Did you know that French women do not wash their hair every day? Yup, it's not so much as wanting to look disheveled but more to retain the naturally produced oils in the hair so the hair is moisturized and also it gives off this tousled look. The ideas are to be comfortable and compatible with having a life but not being too obsessed with looking good and perfect all the time.

13. Perfume is life

French perfumes are known for their high quality, and it is not surprising that French women embody the need to use perfume every time they step out of the house. And why wouldn't they when some of the world's best fragrances are made in France? Perfume forms a significant part of their identity and beauty regime. Also, instead of synthetically made perfumes, they prefer natural scents from flowers and plants.

Conclusion

Ultimately, for the French woman (and man) it is about embracing your uniqueness, freckles and all. To the French, the uniqueness is what makes us all beautiful, but this is a concept that is hard to grasp especially since there seem to be only one or a few types of what the definition of beauty is.

Gapped teeth are beautiful, freckles are beautiful, unruly curly hair is beautiful, and even dark circles are beautiful. The French can be seen as fearless when it comes to their attitude and perception of beauty, preferring to let their flaws show rather than hiding them. While they do put on makeup, it is hardly about covering these flaws rather it is more to make them look fresh and bold. The idea is to use makeup to enhance your best features and reduce whatever flaws you have, but it isn't about looking like a new person entirely.

Less to the chic French woman is more. No super sleek straight hair or puffy blowouts or sharp contouring. The whole look of being French chic is to be fuss-free. While they do put in a lot of effort in their skincare routine, this no doubt is a longer lasting effect rather than piling on tons of makeup.

They practice restraint and balance- put an effort in the things that count and less effort in things that aren't so important. When you think about it, when the basics of healthy skin and hair are achieved, everything else just falls into place naturally. You spend less time fretting about surface issues when the root of the problem has been corrected.

CHAPTER 9:
HOW TO LIVE WITH CONFIDENCE & ELEGANCE

Who comes to your mind when you think about elegance?
Probably Kate Middleton would be a good icon for elegance in the 21st century.

How about confidence? Who comes to your mind when you think this word?

Michelle Obama? Oprah Winfrey? Beyoncé? Kim Kardashian? Aung San Suu Kyi?

All these women embody both elegance as well as confidence.

Elegance in the 21st century is no longer the same as elegance back in the 18th century when women and men walked down cobbled streets dressed in the finest cloth and lace when tables were set in impeccable chinaware, and hot meals in glistening silverware and cultural refinement was a must especially for the upper echelons of society.

But in the world we live now, how would you define elegance and grace for that matter. Women are no longer confined to traditional and conventional gender roles and activities. Instead, women run companies, drive cars, sign checks, run marathons, participate in sports events, compete, go to the gym, cook, clean and yes, breastfeed.

So how would you define elegance in the 21st century?

Honestly, if you look at the iconic women of today, elegance can be defined as how eloquent you are in presenting your ideas, how to hold your own in the face of adversity, helping people from all walks of life and even making this whole world inclusive- this could be the 21st century elegance, and it's mostly derived from how the women of today handle the pressures of being a woman in this day and age.

According to William Hanson, senior etiquette tutor of The English Manner, a modern type finishing school "Being a lady today is about the same principles it always was – there are just different expectations. It's all about elegance and confidence, and the behavior doesn't need to be something straight out of a Jane Austen novel."

Hanson goes on to say that being elegant in the modern world is about having self-respect and also treating other people with respect and having your own personality but not being abrupt about it.

Diana Vreeland once said, "The only real elegance is in our mind; if you've got that, the rest really comes from it."

Diana is right- elegance is a state of mind.

Elegance and confidence are seen very differently around the world and cultures play a big part of how these two traits are defined but ultimately boils down to how a person carries themselves- in the way they speak, in the way they treat other people and also in the way they dress.

Despite what your perceptions or notions may be on what elegance and confidence may be, there are perennial guidelines or elements that the entire world agrees on, and these guidelines are best seen in the French.

How the French radiate elegance and confidence:

No matter how busy your schedule may be or what your daily tasks are, there are plenty of ways to bring in the elegance and confidence in anything you do. Here are some life tips that would be beneficial in helping you create that air of elegance and confidence that you've wanted all along:

- Harness inner peace. An elegant and confident woman radiates inner peace. Mental health and grooming are as important as the physical aspect.
- Have good posture. Maintaining a straight back leads to a more confident posture with your head held high.
- Keep it simple. Statement pieces complement a basic wardrobe.
- Keep meals simple. Simple meals, especially during the weekend help, simplify your life and one that you can whip up at a moment's notice.

- Savor life. This means slowing down and appreciating everything in life.
- No gadgets at the dinner table. Maintaining eye contact and listening to the people sitting with you at a dinner table is good manners.
- Grace and attentiveness tell the person on the other end that you are listening to them and giving them your full attention. It also makes them feel wanted and appreciated.
- Learn the basics of good wine service.
- Keep your nails short and manicured.
- Learn the basics of how to set a table
- Give respect and say thank you, especially to those serving you
- Accept compliments gracefully
- Do more of what comes naturally for you. When you are at ease, you are most elegant
- Tip generously
- Give thoughtful gifts and always send thank you cards
- Not all aspects of your life need to be on social media. Some secrets kept is good to maintain mystery
- Discretion is elegant
- Silence often is better
- Eat in moderation. Don't stuff your plate or yourself
- Enhance your natural beauty by wearing subtle makeup. Don't hide it
- Make an icon your role model. Audrey Hepburn is the ultimate icon for grace, confidence, and elegance. And so are Queen Rania of Jordan, Michelle Obama, and Kate Middleton.
- Use subtle makeup. Enhance your natural beauty, don't try to hide it.
- Find your favorite scent and stick to it. It creates a lasting impression of anyone who knows you and meets you
- Eloquence is key to being elegant. Being loud and obnoxious is rude.
- Thoughtfulness is also an admired trait. Save your swear words for when the time is truly warranted. Some fictional role models you can acquire sass by is through Countess Violet Crawley from Downton Abbey and Lady Olenna Tyrell from Game of Thrones.
- Do not lose your cool in public, unless in extenuating circumstances
- Move gracefully with or without heels
- Adore yourself. Self-loathing and elegance do not mix
- Acquire a sense of humor and wit. Life is boring if it is taken too seriously
- Keep your spaces organized and clean- whether it is your office,

work desk or home.
- Have your dreams
- Live passionately
- Create and maintain boundaries.
- Stand up against people who do not treat you with the respect you deserve
- Read newspapers, magazines, books, the news. Knowing what is happening in the world helps with refined conversation
- Learn French!
- Simplify your life.
- Dress for the job you want, not the job you have
- Sip your drink not guzzle it down
- You are responsible for your own happiness. Nobody can be responsible for that.
- Sip your soup, not slurp it. Unless you're in Japan because that's a sign that you love your food.
- Be grateful even when there is nothing to appreciate at that moment. Life could be much worse.
- Apologize sincerely
- Being elegant isn't about having the most money. Being elegant is a mindset, not your shopping spree
- Always choose quality over quantity
- Travel the world.
- Be confident in who you are, what you are passionate about and what you believe in. Don't let anyone else tell you how to think or act.

These are just some of the ways that you can add confidence and elegance into your life whether in small ways or big ways.

Elegance and confidence is a mind over matter thing. When you think it and practice it, it radiates out of you and people can feel it. That's why sometimes even when watching a movie and you see the character's awkwardness- you can feel it too? The same way confidence is felt through when an actor portrays it. That's how you can feel and exude confidence and elegance.

CHAPTER 10:
MOVIES TO INSPIRE YOUR FASHION
AND SENSE OF PARISIAN CHIC

Apart from who's acting, plenty of movies, sitcoms and dramas become popular due to the wardrobe and fashion the cast wears. Some movies are popular not because of the plot but because of the fashion!
In this list, we will look at memorable movies and the fashion inspiration that we derive from them. They are not particularly French chic but cover different fashion statements and looks depending on what era or time period or century that they are based in. French chic or not, here are some great movies to get your fashion inspiration on!

- **Breakfast at Tiffany's (1961):**

This move is at the top of the list because personally, to me, Audrey Hepburn just kills it acting wise and of course fashion-wise. Her petite frame fits in perfectly into that gorgeous little black dress. The way her hair is made, the makeup she wears, the way she holds her cigarette and that independent spirit of hers is everything a woman wants to be.

You can say that the importance of the little black dress was further emphasized through this movie.

- **La Dolce Vita**

Probably one of the most memorable scenes in this movie is the scene of Anita Ekberg emerging slowly from the Trevi fountain in none other than a black dress. The fact is, this movie was inspired by fashion itself. Director Fellini was quoted saying that it was a sack dress designed by Balenciaga with its dramatic silhouette that inspired the writing and directing of this whole movie.

See what a beautiful dress can do? It can inspire anything!

- **Atonement**

Another fashion moment is that infamous library scene which featured the emerald green silk dress. It was so popular that this dress was copied all over the world and it also made Jacqueline Durran a household name in the world of movie costumes and fashion, for which she was nominated for an Academy Award.

Even though Durran lost out on the Academy Award, her dress was voted by Sky Movies as the best costume of all time.

- **Belle De Jour:**

From figure-hugging pencil skirts to stiletto heels and silk blouses, Catherine Deneuve just knew how to pull of the sexually frustrated housewife character, and the wardrobe helped her morph into this character. The wardrobe for this movie was designed by the iconic Yves Saint Laurent who was roped in to dress Deneuve. Thanks to this collaboration, Yves and Deneuve developed an eternal friendship and became his muse, wearing his designs for her red carpet appearances and future films.

- **Annie Hall (1977):**

Annie Hall is among the popular choices of fashion inspiration. Dianne Keaton's character was dressed impeccably in preppy menswear, and it gave a lasting impression and became the biggest trend when this Woody Allen flick was released. Thanks to this movie, menswear remains a classic look for women looking for that androgynous style.

- **Clueless**

Clueless was both a fashion inspiration and a coming-of-age movie that still remains a popular choice of chick flicks to watch on a lazy night.

Who didn't want to dress like Dionne or Cher with the Alaia mini-dresses, knee-length socks, matchy suits and walk-in wardrobes that made Alicia Silverstone a household name?

There were at least 53 different plaid designs used in the movie, seven of which were worn by Cher and twelve were worn by other characters in the movie.

If nobody remembers the movie, he or she would definitely remember Alicia's performance in Clueless.

- **Cleopatra**

The costumes in Cleopatra may not fit the ideal French chic look, but the movie headlined by Elizabeth Taylor has a striking wardrobe that not only inspired fashion shows all around the world but also makeup trends and accessories.

Most notable to follow the Cleopatra-esque styling was Alexander McQueen's 2007 Autumn/Winter collection.

This film scored a record-breaking budget mainly due to the wardrobe cost that raked in $194,800. This includes a dress made entirely from 24-carat gold cloth. This figure was the highest ever sum to date for one single screen actor.

- **Almost Famous (2000):**

This movie needs to always be in any list concerning fashion movies. Kate Hudson brilliantly portrays the glamorous, whimsical and free-spirited groupie in this film and the outfits designed match this robust personality. Kate Hudson was considered a style icon after this movie and solidified her status as one of Hollywood's A-listers. Thanks to this movie, girls all around the world wanted the Penny-Lane inspired fur-trimmed coat.

- **The Royal Tenenbaums (2001):**

The Royal Tenenbaums directed by Wes Anderson is known for its unique and distinct aesthetic. Of all the characters in the movie, it was Gweneth Paltrow's characters that spawned Halloween costume inspirations.

Her acting together with the outfits went so in sync and made this movie one of the memorable fashion inspirations. Not only the outfits that were popular, but it was also the entire film setting that makes this movie a visually appealing and entertaining feature.

- **The Great Gatsby**

If you are looking for inspiration on flapper styles, watch the Great Gatsby. This list would not be complete without the Jazz Age inspiration of Daisy dressed in white, the head pieces, and the glamorous décor. Whether it is the 1920s version or the 2013 version, the Great Gatsby is memorable for the characters, the storyline and above all the fashion and the décor of 1920's New York.

- **Pretty Woman**

Julia Robert's character in Pretty Woman has some of the most iconic looks. Despite playing a prostitute, Julia Robert's Vivian had some of the most memorable looks such as the brown polka dot ensemble to the off shoulder red dress.

- **Lolita**

This was a controversial movie as epitomizes the sexualizing of a young girl. Based on the novel of the same name, Lolita showcased a powerful storyline and also inspired the pop culture reference to the name Lolita, to mean grown women acting in a child-like manner. From the heart-shaped and cat-shaped sunglasses to the off shoulder tops, this movie inspired many a Halloween costumes for the kinky.

Thanks to Lolita, it garnered a large sub-culture movement in Japan where all things kinky prevail.

- **The Seven Year Itch**

This is another iconic movie with the most infamous photograph of Marilyn Monroe in that beautiful and sexy white halter-neck dress billowing around her legs as she stands cheekily over a subway grating. This shot was originally taken on Lexington Avenue in Manhattan. The Seven Year Itch dress was also a dress that spawned many copycats.

While Marilyn was taking these shots, the crowd of onlookers cheered and whistled. This made Marilyn miss her lines. The scene had to be reshot again in a studio with no interruptions.

And what happened to the dress? It was recently sold off at an auction for $4.6 million dollars.

- **Basic Instinct**

Apart from Marilyn's iconic white dress, another dress that goes down in the history of sexy dresses would be Sharon Stone's all white skin tight outfit in the unforgettable scene of Basic Instinct.

If you thought only a black dress had the power to do that, well Sharon Stone proved everyone wrong. Thanks to this scene and that dress, she was instantly famous.

This white dress was created by Ellen Mirojnick from scratch. Ellen was quoted saying that she wanted Sharon's character, Catherine to resemble an 'ice blonde' that was similar to a 'Hitchcockian character'.

- *Grease* (1978)

What is not to love about Grease? Again this may not be your Parisian chic style but who can say no to the 50s vibe of skirt and sweater combo. The whole oversized sweater look the French wore was probably inspired by Grease!

Sandy's transformation from innocent girl-next-door to sexy leather-clad rocker chic is an iconic moment for anyone who watches this movie.

- **The Devil Wears Prada**

My personally favorite, The Devil Wears Prada is also a must in fashion lists. This movie adapted from Lauren Weisberger's bestselling novel based on her real-life experience as a PA to none other than US Vogue editor-in-chief Anna Wintour made the title character, Anne Hathaway an instant star.

Both Anne Hathaway's character Andy and Meryl Streep's silver-haired character Miranda Priestly donned designer garments that many designers lent their clothes and accessories. The wardrobe itself was overseen by Patricia Field who is also the guru of style behind Sex & the City.

The Devil Wears Prada became one of the most expensively costumed movies, and surprise, surprise – Anna Wintour herself lived it. She attended the screening wearing Prada from head to toe. This movie also earned Meryl Streep her 14th Oscar nomination as the demanding and ruthless boss to Andy.

- **Sex and the City: The Movie (2008):**

Speaking of Sex and the City, this list ends with none other than the mother of all fashion movies. This is a classic that has spawned plenty of copycat fashions. Women everywhere wanted to be like them and dress like them.

Sex and the City movie is exactly like it is drama on TV- full of fashionable clothes, shoes, sunglasses, bags, and scarves that gives you plenty of inspiration. From NYC style to Parisian chic to Arabian boldness, all the four main characters personified their character's personality through their fashion sense.

SOPHIE CLAIRE

CONCLUSION

Thank you for taking time to read this book. Hopefully, the ideas and guidelines presented in this book will help you get one step closer to achieving your dream and purpose in dressing like the chic French women. These guidelines will also help you in living your life with confidence and elegance.
Sometimes, a little change in our wardrobe or the way we present ourselves can do wonders for our lifestyle. It can take it from boring to amazing with a few simple style changes and gives us a different outlook on life.

Fashion has that power to do it, and as witnessed in Breakfast at Tiffany's, a little black dress can definitely change the world.

OTHER BOOKS BY SOPHIE CLAIRE

French Chic: 21 French Style Lessons To Dress Chic And Look Charming

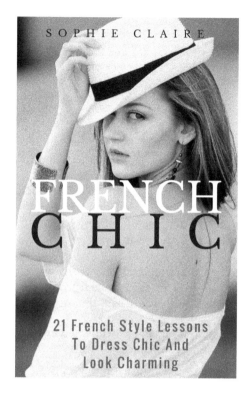

Did you know that French women look on average 7 years younger than British women? Have you ever wondered "how do they do it?". Imagine if you knew the style secrets of a Parisian woman. Imagine if you could dress French chic and look gorgeous everyday. Effortlessly.
We all know. Putting together the right outfit can be such a hassle. The truth is, French women look so gorgeous because of their own style secrets.

In French fashion there are so many little known tips and tricks that drastically improve the way you look. Dressing elegantly like a French woman has its own rules. Once you learn them, putting together amazing French chic outfits will be easy. But don't worry.

Being chic doesn't mean dressing in a boring and dull way. That is not the essence of French chic. This book is a guide to create your own unique fashion signature.

In this book you'll learn exactly how to dress and look French chic. You will find 21 easy-to-follow French style lessons that will teach you all the secrets of the chicest Parisian women. Every lesson you'll read is geared towards a particular area of fashion and beauty. You'll discover how easy it is to look gorgeous and, most important, feel confident and beautiful.

Some French Chic Lessons You'll Discover In The Book:
- 9 Fashion Items You Must Add To Your Wardrobe
- How To Pair Your Outfit The Right Way
- 8 Fashion Errors To Avoid (Most People Don't Know Them)
- How To Dress According To Your Unique Body Shape
- French Chic's Best Colors And Fabrics
- Skincare And Makeup Advice
- How To Get Dressed Parisian Chic
- What Things Are French Chic And What Aren't
- French Style's Guide To Choose The Best Lingerie
- How To Choose Footwear And Accessories
- And much, much more

Stop dreaming about being fashion. Buy this book today and start living French chic.

"French Chic" is available at Amazon.

Capsule Wardrobe: Discover Your Personal Style And Create Your Dream Wardrobe

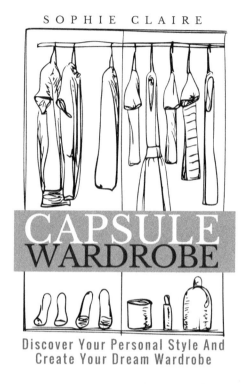

Discover how to create countless outfits from less than 50 clothing items

Have you ever tried to search for the right outfit in a hurry? Imagine being late for an appointment. You open your wardrobe and always feel overwhelmed by the number of items. Unless you have an outfit already in your mind, you start opening drawers, carefully scanning all the hangers, throwing clothes on your bed in an attempt to see what items could fit well together. Does this sound familiar?

Now just imagine you were able to open your wardrobe and clearly see all the items inside it with just a few glances. Imagine if you could just pick up two items already knowing they'll fit well together.

Creating a capsule wardrobe can solve all these clothing problems, and the best part is you don't have to trash all your clothes and buy new expensive items. If you're looking for a way to simplify and improve your wardrobe you've come to the right place.

A capsule wardrobe is based on the concept of creating a combination of versatile items that can fit together in endless combinations.

Imagine if you could create countless outfits with less than 50 items in your closet.

So many women have already created their unique capsule wardrobe, and they love it, because a mini wardrobe it's practical, effective and can also help you save time and money.

With the right guide you will be able to discover your own unique style and create a perfect capsule wardrobe in a matter of days. However, you can't just put together 10 t-shirts, 10 trousers and 5 pairs of shoes *to create the perfect capsule wardrobe.* You need to stick to some guidelines.

This book will teach you everything you need to know to simplify your closet and create your own capsule wardrobe following your unique fashion style. You'll discover that wasting money on sale items you'll simply never wear isn't the solution to look charming.

You'll learn:
- How To Choose Clothes Based On Your Silhouette
- Basic Items Every Woman Should Have In Her Wardrobe
- Capsule Wardrobe Rules To Organize And Pair Your Clothes
- Two Types Of Accessories For Everyone
- How and When To Update Your Wardrobe
- How To Choose The Right Colors For Your Complexion
- A Shopping Guide To Buy New Clothes Without Cluttering Your Wardrobe
- What Colors You Need In Your Capsule Wardrobe
- Seasonal Maintenance Tips
- Clever Tips To Simplify And Improve Your Wardrobe
- And much, much more

Simplify your wardrobe today!

"Capsule Wardrobe" is available at Amazon.

CPSIA information can be obtained
at www.ICGtesting.com
Printed in the USA
LVHW081949050421
683466LV00009B/634